MW00935957

Struggles to Victory
Over Racism in America

Canaan Kennedy

First published by Canaan Kennedy in 2015
© Canaan Jacob Leon Kennedy
All rights reserved. Any of the contents and images
cannot be duplicated unless written permission is
given from the publisher.

Canaan Kennedy
111 Meadow Rue Ct.
Williamsburg, VA 23185
canaankennedy@gmail.com
www.strugglestovictory.com

ISBN: 978 1508407799
ISBN: 1508407797

Cover design by Dori Kennedy
Printed in the United States

CONTENTS

Father Adam, Canaan and brother Jacob.

Preface
Canaan Jacob Leon Kennedy

I begin with a quote from James Baldwin's film The Price of the Ticket: "Some days - and this is one of them - you wonder what your role is in this country and what your future is in it?"

My name is Canaan Jacob Leon Kennedy. I am seventeen years old and a biracial child. My mother is white and my father is black. I grew up in mostly white Williamsburg, Virginia where over eighty percent of the people are white. We live in a house in the woods, seeming like we are isolated from the world. My father, Adam P. Kennedy, is the only black person in our neighborhood.

As a child I would tell the other kids in my elementary school that I was half black, but they wouldn't believe me, questioning my identity. Everyone thought I was white because I have a fair skin tone. When my father would come pick me up from class the kids would say, "That's not your dad," and "Who is that?", not accepting that my father was black. I can remember many times having to bring in pictures of my father and family to class to prove to my classmates that I wasn't a liar. This continuous bombardment of disbelief and disapproval of my being half black caused me a great deal of emotional and social troubles through the years. I struggled with who I was and what my true identity was; I felt as if I didn't belong anywhere because I was this mixed race - something, someone different than those around me. For a while I thought that being different than my peers was a bad thing because different is strange, but through these experiences and learning of my family's history, I have learned to embrace my black side and to always strive to hold my head high when expressing who I am.

My mother, Renee Kennedy, and my father own a publishing company and have worked at home for my entire life. For years I would watch my father at his desk while he wrote, working on screenplays, books and ideas. My mother is an accomplished painter and her works are displayed in homes across America. She was always working on new artwork. She is also part owner of the New Town art gallery in Williamsburg, Virginia.

I have an older sister, Dori, who is white. My mother was pregnant with Dori when she met my father. She was recently widowed: her husband was killed in a car accident. My parents had three children together, myself and my two younger brothers, Jacob and Caleb. Because my father worked at home he would always have time for his children, helping us with homework and attending our school events. Every night my mother would cook dinner and my siblings and I would sit around the dinner table and then my father would start speaking about our black ancestors, global icons and people who have changed the world for the better. Every night would be something different, a new lesson about life. He would make us write reports and speeches on great historical figures such as Mahatma Gandhi, Malcolm X, Harriet Tubman and Patrice Lumumba. We had to prepare speeches to be presented to the family every weekend. We would have to stand in the center of the living room, standing up straight and speaking loudly. My father would critique us and give us a letter grade. If you were given a poor grade on/for your speech then we would have to redo it the following week along with the new assignment. At first I didn't look forward to these events, but after a while I started seeing it as a competition with my siblings and I didn't want to lose - that is in my nature. This exercise definitely enhanced my public speaking abilities. In school I was always active in debates, never holding back to express my opinions. Now that I look back on it, I want to truly thank him for forcing us to give speeches because it taught me so much about the world and gave me this confidence to speak in front of people, whether it's a job interview, a regular conversation or a speech.

My parents have influenced me a great deal through talking with them and learning from their success and failures. I never really thanked them for all the wisdom they have given me. Perhaps, through this book I can finally thank them for everything.

I come from a family of visionaries and entrepreneurs. My grandfather, Dr. Joseph C. Kennedy, was a co-founder of *Africare*, a non-profit organization he started in 1973. The company still operates today, and he's still active as the Secretary on the Board of Directors. *Africare* works to improve the quality of life for the people in Africa while also improving relations between the people of Africa and black Americans.

My grandmother, Adrienne Kennedy, is a world renowned playwright. Her most distinguished plays include *Funnyhouse of a Negro, Ohio State Murders and The Lennon Play: In His Own Write.* She has taught at Harvard, Stanford and Yale. She was apart of the Black Arts movement in the 1960s and 1970s, her plays are taught at universities all around the world. Adrienne Kennedy was awarded the Anisfield-Wolf Lifetime Achievement Award and was nominated by the Theatre for a New Audience for the Nobel Peace Prize.

My father has always wanted to be a writer. He has written plays, novels and screenplays, and he started his own publishing house. My mother and father have always worked side by side creating their publishing company. This has had a big affect on my outlook on life and how I want to make a living, not wanting to work for anyone, but rather build something out of my own inspiration and creative ideas. I see my family developing careers and businesses out of what they love and it inspires me to do the same.

My grandfather always wanted to go to Africa and make a lasting impact on people who were less fortunate than he. *Africare* did just that. His NGO - Non-Governmental Organization has saved lives, improved the quality of life for millions. I often wonder if I can live up to his legacy? Will I be able to affect as many people as he has. Perhaps not, but I will strive towards achieving great heights as he has. I hope to find what it is I love and make something out of it, so that my life can be as fulfilled as theirs are.

I believe childhood experiences shape who we become as adults. As a child I traveled to New York City to see my grandmother, Adrienne Kennedy who lived on the Upper West Side of Manhattan. I remember my father and I walking through the streets of New York visiting the various museums, going to the Empire State building, walking through the Columbia University campus where my grandfather worked tirelessly to get his PhD. I have always loved New York City; it has strange appeal to me and to millions. All of the famous actors and musicians came there. They all walked the streets of this great city. I hope to be a star like them one day.

During the summer of my middle-school years we took a vacation to Hawaii, to the island of Kauai. It was the most beautiful place I had ever seen, the water was so clear and blue, the weather was always amazing. We rented a house on this little beach and went swimming every morning. We stayed for about seven weeks. I enjoyed every moment of it. We went to a luau, we went snorkeling, we rode on sea turtles and went on a boat ride around the island. We had so much fun we decided to go again the following year. It was the first time I can remember being surrounded by people of color, Hawaiians, Polynesians and Asians. This had a powerful and inspirational effect on me, seeing people of color in positions of authority running and controlling a diverse community. When I settle down with a family I want my children to live in an environment with ethnic and cultural diversity.

Growing up I didn't see as much of my mother's family as compared to my father's family. I don't know as much about their lives compared to my father's family. Virtually all of my mother's family was born, raised and still lives in Pennsylvania. My mother's mother, Sandra Flock, died of cancer, and my grandfather, Henry Flock, lives in Finleyville, Pennsylvania. I only have fond memories from visiting Pennsylvania and my mother's family was always so kind to me. We don't see them as often but that doesn't diminish the love and respect I have for them. I see my father's side more often because they live closer.

My Inspiration

The summer of 2014, Ferguson, Missouri was in the news. I thought a lot about Michael Brown and it made me think about race in America. Black Americans have been oppressed and put down by our white society and it is a shame that something like the murder of Michael Brown finally compels the media to talk about race in America. Racism is the one topic that white Americans hate to talk about. Nobody wants to talk negatively of their race but the horrific events of the past can't be ignored as if they never existed.

The institution of slavery and the imperialistic ways of America are rarely spoken of because it puts America in a bad light, and Americans don't want to recognize the true history of their nation - a nation built off the backs of African slaves, land taken from Native Americans, entire tribes nearly exterminated off the face of the planet by European Americans. These thoughts swirled around my mind that summer.

While these events were taking place I was reading James Baldwin's *Notes of a Native Son*. I admire Baldwin and he inspired me to try to write about race in America and around the world. These factors influenced me to talk to my family about their experiences dealing with the racism black people have to face living in America. I wanted to learn about my family's struggles and victories so that I could better understand how to navigate my life better, and I wanted to give people an insight into how to combat racism. I hope that this book can mean something to others, and help teach people what I have learned, that no matter what difficulties we may face in life, we can always overcome and achieve success. People will always try to bring you down, but that can not deter you from reaching new heights and becoming a success. You can be anything that you want to be don't let anyone tell you otherwise. This book is focused on understanding how the black members of my family faced and overcame racism in America.

Canaan Kennedy in London, England 2015.

My father Adam P. Kennedy and my Mother Renee Kennedy.

Joe Jr. Adam P. and Dr. Joseph Kennedy With President Carter.

Chapter I
Adam Patrice Kennedy

Growing up my father would tell me and my siblings stories of his experiences with racism, being a black kid in New York and London. He had all white peers and classmates and he frequently got into fights and was beaten up. I can remember sitting at the dinner table while he discussed his experiences with racism. When he was living in London as a child he was the only black kid, and he was ostracized because he looked different than the other kids. He recalls being chased and beaten up by two white brothers everyday after school. His mother would wait for him at the door with a broomstick to deter the brothers.

While my father and grandmother were living in Manhattan, New York City, my father attended Manhattan Country school during junior high and then attended Riverdale, a prestigious high school in the Bronx, New York. Most of the students at Riverdale were white and came from rich or upper

-class families. My father got along with most of the kids at his high school but they definitely didn't understand the black experience or the middle class black American. Most of the students at Riverdale lived in the affluent areas of the Upper East and West Side of Manhattan. They were picked up everyday by private school buses and driven to Riverdale through Harlem and Spanish Harlem, (on the upper West and East sides of Manhattan) which at that time the residents were poor blacks and Hispanics. The brownstones and tenements of the area were battered and abandoned. With little interaction with people of color this must have had a profound effect on the minds of the mostly white students at Riverdale.

While in high school my father became a star athlete playing football and running track. My father was extremely fast but he had weak knees, so at track meets he would literally hobble down to the blocks and slowly get into his stance and then he would bolt off - winning nearly every race. He ran the 100 and 220 yard dash and the long jump. He was a track star at Riverdale but he never had a real coach to teach him how to run properly and to learn the different techniques to get a faster time.

In his junior year he decided to forego playing football and focus solely on track. This displeased the football coach because he was one of their top players. With his mind on track he practiced hard and won every meet he ran. On a road meet against a rival school, he won the 100 yard dash running the fastest time in Riverdale history. After the meet was over they went back to the school and informed the athletic director of the new record. The athletic director told my father that his time was not valid because it was during a road meet and they were not going to recognize his time. The athletic director told my father that all the records were home records. When pressed about the reasoning for not getting the record my father has told me that resentment and race were certainly factors. Many of the sprint records were twenty years old and were held by a school icon who was white. My father had worked hard for three years to break those records, and when he finally achieved the ultimate goal, there was no recognition of it because he was black.

After graduating from Riverdale he enrolled at Antioch College. At Antioch he received a double major in Journalism and International Studies. Soon after graduating he started looking for a job. After searching around he finally landed one at Time Warner Books in New York City. On his application it said that he was born in Rome, Italy, and the president of the division my father worked in at the time was Italian. He was qualified for the position but the major reason he got the job over others was because he was presumed to be Italian. After a couple weeks working there the president asked, how the new Italian hire was doing. They pointed to my father and the president said, "He's not Italian, he's black." Luckily for my father they didn't fire him because he had proved that he was capable of doing the job. In this instance racial/ethnic bias worked out in his favor. This happens in the workplace often; someone is hired solely because of their gender or ethnicity, which is wrong, but it clearly happens. It is unfair to the person who doesn't get the job, but I don't think there's a way for racial or gender discrimination to end because it is so difficult to prove.

Anyways, while advancing at Time Warner my father worked on special projects for the president, bringing in new ideas and increasing profitability. An important job opened up as the assistant to the vice president of one of the major book divisions. The president thought that my father could bring new energy to a division that was struggling. The vice president was a man who was openly racist and deeply resented the president assigning my father to him. The vice president looked for ways to fire my father despite the division's improvement. The vice president asked him to work on a special project that required my father to work overtime. At the time overtime pay was frozen and any overtime work had to be authorized by the vice president or president. Unauthorized overtime was a fireable offense. The vice president told my father that he had authorized his overtime and when my father turned in his time sheet showing over forty hours of overtime the vice president had the ammunition to fire my father. Racism had cost him an opportunity to continue working for Time Warner.

My father has dealt with his fair share of racist circumstances throughout his years. The worst experience he endured was when he was beaten up by a police officer outside of his father's home in the predominantly white neighborhood of Arlington, Virginia. He was driving to my grandfather's house late at night with one of his friends who was black. The officer had followed them in his patrol car with his lights off for several miles. My grandfather's house sits at the end of steep dead end street that leads into a park. There are no lamp posts lining the street so at night it is very dark. Half way down the steep hill the officer turned on his front lights and overhead lights. My father was startled by the sudden lights and continued down the hill pulling into his father's driveway. The officer got out of his car yelling at my father, proceeding to hit my father with his flashlight, knocking him to the ground. He kicked and punched him in the face and body knocking him almost unconscious. My father was yelling and screaming, "What have I done?!", as the officer dragged him across the driveway to his patrol car. Other police officers arrived on the scene as my grandfather, step-grandmother and uncle came out of the house horrified to see what was happening to my father. The officers on the scene drew their guns pointing them at my family, shouting at them to "Get back!" "What are his charges?!" they yelled. "What has he done?!" They threw my father and his friend into the back of a police wagon and took them to the precinct where they were handcuffed to a bench. They were released on bail a couple hours later.

The arresting officer charged my father with assault and if convicted he would go to jail. My father was a graduate of Antioch College, he had spend a semester at Princeton and had never been charged with a crime in his life. The Kennedy family's first step was to get a lawyer. They went to the NAACP for a recommendation. They spoke to a black lawyer and she suggested for him to plead guilty. She asked my father if he had ever been in trouble and if they were on drugs he replied "No." She whispered to him "It's okay, I know your parents are here but you can tell me the truth." He was outraged; she didn't believe his story. He walked out of that office that day thinking he was going to jail.

Still in search of a capable lawyer, my grandmother, Adrienne Kennedy called up a friend who suggested Roger Adelman, a renowned lawyer and former U.S District Attorney. The family hired Mr. Adelman to represent my father and he was confident that the Arlington County District Attorney's office didn't have a case. There was no evidence that my father assaulted the officer. He coached my father in what to say and how to say it so that the DA couldn't make a case against him. The judge at the trial, after hearing three police officers testify had heard enough and acquitted my father of all charges.

Throughout the whole ordeal my father had been writing down his thoughts and recollections of what happened. My grandmother, Adrienne Kennedy had also been writing down her thoughts. Together they combined what they had and in a couple of months they had written a full-length play, *Sleep Deprivation Chamber*. They sent it to James Houghton, a producer and theatrical pioneer who, with an ingenious idea of single-playwright seasons, did the imposs -ible: he created a theatrical empire with Signature Theatre. James Houghton loved the play and Michael Kahn, one of the foremost stage directors of our time directed it. He has taught at Juilliard and directed plays for the Shakespeare Theatre Company. It is said that he has this power which he translates into images that makes performances magical. Nobody understand actors better than Michael Kahn. *Sleep Deprivation Chamber* was performed in New York at the Public Theater, and it received good reviews in the New York Times and was soon named Best New American Play by the Village Voice OBIE's, Off Broadway Theatre Awards.

Adam accepting the 1996, Best New American Play Obie Award for *Sleep Deprivation Chamber*.

Here is an excerpt from my interview with my father, Adam P. Kennedy, concerning his incident with the police. Conducted on August 20th, 2014 at Canaan Kennedy's home in Williamsburg, Virginia.

Canaan: How did *Sleep Deprivation Chamber* come about?

Adam P. Kennedy: *Sleep Deprivation* came about from when I was stopped by the police and beaten up by this police officer. That's how it came about.

Canaan: Can you go into detail about that?

Adam P. Kennedy: Okay, 1991. I was staying with Grandpapa and Claire's. They're in Arlington, VA. Duane Grier, one of my good friends from college, came over and we went out; it was a Saturday night if I remember correctly and Duane and I hung out pretty regularly on the weekends and we went out to a bar, several bars that we usually went to. Then, we were heading back, we were driving Grandpapa's car. It was a green Ford Granada. We were in the district, in DC, and on occasion, Duane would stay the night. So on this occasion, he came back with me, it was probably about 2 o'clock in the morning and we stopped at an all night diner called Bob and Edith's, I've shown it to you. It's right across the street from William Jefferies where we now go to have oysters.

We stopped there and we had breakfast and then we drove back to the house. That's only a couple of minutes. As you know, on Grandpapa's and Claire's street, it's very dark. So by the time I was half way - more than halfway down the hill, I was surprised, stunned, that all of a sudden there were these police lights. Red and blue lights flashing. I had no idea where they were coming from. He was right behind us. I pulled into Grandpapa's driveway and he pulled in behind us and I got out of the car, I actually started walking into the house, not really necessarily realizing he was dealing with us because I couldn't figure out why the lights were on. I started walking to the house, as did Duane, and the officer said, "Get back in the car." And I stopped and I said, "Officer, I live here."

I said, "What seems to be the problem?" Again, he said to me, "Get back in the car." And I said to him, I repeated, "Officer, I live here, what seems to be the problem?" Maybe that happened one more time. So finally, he said, "Get back in the car." So I made my way back to the car. And still asking, "What seems to be the problem?" This was in January, so it was cold. I went to get back in the car, I opened the car door and he said, "Come back here." I'm a little nervous because he was agitated. Duane was still by the passenger side door. I was wearing a heavy jacket and again, I sensed he was a little bit agitated. He had the flashlight in his hand. He was shining it in my face. I had several other experiences with the police that made me very fearful of the police.. So I listened to what he said and I walked back to him and we got pretty close to each other when all of a sudden I was hit in the side of the head. He hit me in the head with his flashlight and knocked me to the ground.

He then proceeded to kick and punch me and then drag me. At that point we were near the end of the car. He dragged me across the driveway and threw me to the ground. In retrospect, at that time, Grandpapa and Claire had a row of large rocks lining the driveway. I didn't know it then, but when he threw me to the ground, my head just missed one of these big rocks. He threw me to the ground, he's kicking me, he's beating me. Duane is yelling and I'm sort of out of it. I wasn't unconscious but I was pretty well dazed. The next thing I remember is a number of other police cars, two, three, four other police cars were there with other officers coming out. At this point Dad and Claire and Uncle Joe, who was at the house, came out of the house. Grandpa and Claire were in their pajamas. And the officers - I'll never forget that - several of the officers withdrew their guns and they were pointing their guns at Grandpapa and Claire and Joe very menacingly.

I'm trying to remember the sequence of events. A couple of officers picked me up and they slammed me spread eagle on the front of the squad car and one of them was holding me down pretty hard. I was screaming. I said, "I'm an American citizen, what have I done?" Then, Duane was saying to one of the officers, this black officer, "What are you doing?" She said, "Shut up, keep your mouth quiet. Keep quiet. If you say anything else I'm going to arrest you." He said, "I can ask a question." And then she went over, she grabbed him and she put the handcuffs on him. Then, Dad is yelling, "What's going on? What has he done?" I don't know, there were six, seven, eight officers on the scene. Lights flashing. Again, their guns were drawn - several of them had their guns drawn. I kept asking, "What have I been arrested for? What have I done?" No one answered me.

A few minutes later they threw Duane and me into the back of a paddy wagon. I could hear Dad yelling, "What has he done?" And no one would answer him. Uncle Joe had a video camera and he had been videotaping some of this when he came out. I'm sure he'll show it to you if you want to see it. It doesn't have a lot, it's kind of frantic. Then we got taken to the precinct. I was badly beaten up. They handcuffed us, they took us inside; they handcuffed us to a bench and one of the police doctors or a paramedic was examining me and he said "He's been pretty well beaten up." We just were there sitting on the bench, handcuffed.

I don't know how much time elapsed, a hour, two hours, when Grandpapa and Claire and Joe arrived. They had been trying to get us released and I think there was like a thousand dollar bond on each one of us. And since it was a Saturday night, Grandpapa didn't have an ATM card. It just happened to be that mum, Mrs. Hunken, Claire's mother, had $2,000 in cash at the house. We were released on bail and I was charged with assaulting a police officer and Duane was charged with resisting arrest. After Grandpa and Claire picked us up, they took me to the hospital where I was examined. All the doctors said, "He's been pretty well beaten up." My face was messed up, my mouth, luckily nothing broken, but I had been kicked in the chest and punched all over my body and that was that part of it.

Canaan: Okay. How did you prepare for the trial, who was your lawyer?

Adam P. Kennedy: The next day, Grandmama came from New York and I guess they consulted on what to do and a lawyer was recommended from the NAACP. Your grandparents, Duane and myself met with the lawyer. She was a black woman. She said, "Okay, tell me what happened." We told her what happened. She said, "You've been charged with assaulting an officer, this is a very serious crime." She suggested right off the bat that we plead guilty and get a reduced charge. Both Duane and I said, "No. There's no way we're doing that." Everyone agreed. I said, "I've never been in trouble." Then, I'll never forget, she looked at me and she stared at me and smirked. And she said, "You can tell me the truth, I know your parents are here but you can tell me the truth." I was totally offended. She just assumed that we had been in trouble before. I knew right then and there that she wasn't the right person. She didn't believe us.

She painted a pretty bleak picture and I left that office feeling that I was going to go to jail. Lorton Prison is only about twenty minutes, a half hour from Arlington; I passed it a zillion times coming down to Williamsburg. I was scared.

Then, Adrienne (Grandmama) contacted a friend who recommended a lawyer in the district. His firm was Kirkpatrick and Lockhart. That's where we met the person who ended up taking on my case, his name is Roger M. Adelman.

Canaan: How did you prepare for the trial? What advice did he give you?

Adam P. Kennedy: Roger Adelman. He was a very highly regarded lawyer. He was a former US district attorney. He had prosecuted John Hinckley, the man who shot President Reagan. He's done many other things. He was a very noted trial attorney.

There were a variety of things going on at the time. I was doing our TV show, *Africa/USA: The Connrction*, and *The World Connection* and at some point, the whole Rodney King incident - I'm sure you're familiar with - happened as well. I had gotten a nice article in the Washington Post about the TV show and there was a debate on whether we should take this to the press or not. Roger, to his credit, said "No, let's not do that."

Grandmama got quite a few people to write letters on my behalf. I think in some ways, it made the Arlington County's District Attorney's office very angry. In their minds we were a typical uneducated poor black family. When they started getting letters from the governor's office, former governors, prominent individuals, they realized that they had messed with the wrong black family. But instead of being cooperative, it made them angrier and they dug in their heels more.

The first time Roger and myself met with the Arlington district attorney, it was pretty evident right from the bat that this wasn't much of a case. He just assumed that she was going to drop it but she didn't. She said, "This is going to trial." Roger was very surprised because there was no evidence that I had struck this officer.

Anyway, the main thing Roger emphasized was just being calm, telling the truth and making sure your story is always the same. He tried to get it thrown out but they wouldn't do it. We went to trial and other people who are testifying can't be in the court room. So Grandmama didn't want to be there, I can't remember why. But Uncle Joe and Duane and Grandpapa and Claire weren't allowed to be in the courtroom because they were witnesses. The officer who beat me, his name was Officer Castro. He was a light skinned Latino.

Canaan: There was a police training book on how officers should deal with different races?

Adam P. Kennedy: That's later on. That was when the civil case adjudicated. We found out, the second officer on the scene was a black woman. She was the first person to draw her gun. She got on the stand first and said, "The accused were erratic and behaving angrily", and they "had no choice but to draw their guns", and so on and so forth.

Roger was able to dismiss her pretty quickly. Another officer got on the stand. He had gotten there late and he didn't have much to say so he couldn't corroborate Officer Castro's testimony. Officer Castro finally got on the stand and we learned that officer Castro had followed us from Bob and Edith's. My car had a broken tail light which we didn't know about until during the trial.

As Roger grilled the officer, he made it clear that Castro could have stopped us anytime on Columbia Pike, the whole mile and a half before we go up the hill to inform us that we had a broken tail light. He said he didn't do that because he wanted to see what else we were going to do. Roger just pounced on that. He said, "What do you mean what else they're going to do?" He said, "They had a broken tail light, why didn't you stop them for a broken tail light?" He was following us. He claimed he didn't know we were black. At that time, Arlington was predominantly white. He followed us with his lights off for a mile and a half. He claimed that once we got down to the bottom of the hill he was frightful because I hadn't stopped and we were heading toward the house. As I said, it's something I've done a zillion times, got out of the car, walked to the house. Anyway, he then proceeded to say what happened. He admitted he hit me in the head with the flashlight. The reason he hit me in the head was because I apparently brushed him, I brushed his lapel. First he said I hit him and then again Roger pressed him. Roger said, "Did Mr. Kennedy hit you with his fist?" He said, "No." Roger asked, "Was his hand opened?" He said, "Yes." Roger said, "Was it forceful enough to knock you back?" "No." He replied. Roger asked him "Mr. Kennedy didn't touch you at all did he?" I remember vividly Officer Castro lost his temper and he said "He touched me. I don't like to be touched."

Roger went into this whole thing, "As a police officer you're trained to contain violence and have appropriate response. Beating Mr. Kennedy to a pulp does not seem like an appropriate response." The officer was angry and irritated, his story was crumbling. After Roger finished cross examining him, the judge, to her credit, said, "I've heard enough and based on the evidence I've heard, this does not constitute assaulting a police officer. The case is dismissed." I was in shock. Happily so. I looked at Roger and he said, "That's it, it's over. We won." I came running out of the courtroom with my hands held high. I said, "We've won!" It was fantastic.

Everything the officers had said had been a lie. That was the end of the criminal case and then Roger suggested that there was a civil case here. So, Roger and - I can't remember the other lawyers name now - we decided to sue Arlington County for damages, for pain and suffering. This went on for months; it was a very arduous situation.

In the civil case, we were allowed to go to the courthouse and the police department and go through their files. Tom Foltz, he was the other lawyer, very good. Tom stumbled upon the training manual for Arlington county police. It was as racist as you could get. It talked about how police officers should interact with different races of people. To paraphrase, "You deal with white people in a more respectful way. They tend to be calmer and more law obedient. Black people are more rambunctious and rowdy and disrespectful of the law so you have to be more forceful with them." It was horrible. We found something that was very important and that really was a testament to how the Arlington county police were trained. Arlington county is pretty liberal when you consider all the other counties around it. So, that was very disturbing.

I forgot to mention in the trial, when Roger asked officer Castro where he was currently employed, he said "The US Secret Service." He had quit his job as an Arlington county police officer, probably forced out, but he got another job with the secret service which says whatever it says. Later on we learned that he was forced to quit because he had a previous experience working for the Arlington Police force where he had harassed or beaten up a black woman so it was time for him to go.

Canaan: How did you come up with *Sleep Deprivation Chamber?*

Adam P. Kennedy: I decided I wanted to capture that evening, that period. At the time we were doing television and I thought this might make an interesting story, after Rodney King, and I had so many interactions with black men who had had very bad experiences with the police. I had already had several other encounters that were nearly as bad. I decided to write down what happened. I gave those pages to Grandmama (Adam's mother, Adrienne Kennedy) and she had been working on her thoughts about what had happened to me and to the family. It's to her credit, she put them together and we liked what we had. She decided to see if she could get someone to get interested in it. It was her impulse. The play, you've never seen it, it's sort of part realistic courtroom drama which is what I wrote, then there's this surreal world that she wrote that deals with the anxiety and the anger and the persecution of a family.

It was 1995 - 1996. Your grandmother was offered the Signature Theatre Season. Jim Houghton was doing something very unique which was presenting a whole year of a playwright's work. He liked *Sleep Deprivation Chamber* and wanted to include it in her season. He chose Michael Kahn who is a fantastic director. He had done your grandmother's first play *Funnyhouse of A Negro.*

He came from Washington D.C to direct it and he did a fantastic job. Then subsequently, it got a very good review in the New York Times; it was wonderful. It got good reviews in a number of other papers and subsequently it was nominated for Best New American Play by the Village Voice Obie's Association and it won Best New American Play. That was quite an honor to receive the award. I've always wanted to work with my mother, so that was very special. And the two of us on stage together, it was wonderful.

Canaan: Can you explain that night that you accepted the award?

Adam P. Kennedy: I think it was a little bit surreal. Again, you go from being beaten up and like I said, if the officer had - when he dragged me across the driveway, as he was kicking me and punching me - when he threw me to the ground, if my head had landed another four or five inches to the left he might have cracked my skull and I would have been dead. To turn that horrible event, to have the police pointing their guns at Grandpapa and Claire, and Joe and all the things they put us through ... I truly believe that if we had been a white family in the same upper middle class position, they would have dropped the charges. I do believe that once they found out that we were prominent, I think they were going to show us, "You don't come into our house and tell us what to do. We're sending you to jail." I think that's become more obvious over the years. That the letters and the phone calls, not just from average people, but from lawyers and professors and the governor's office, the senator's office would have persuaded them to drop the case. Most people would have said, let's look at the case, it's flimsy and we're going to dismiss it. But they dug their heels in. I'll never forget, when the judge dismissed the case, the head district attorney, he storm -ed out of the courtroom. He was furious; he was furious.

That night was a combination of - it was surreal. It was also an honor to be able to do something with my mother because I've always wanted to do that.

This is an example of overcoming a difficult situation and making the best of it. It pains me to think that my father, the nicest, most genuine person I know would have to go through something like this. It infuriates me that this can happen to black men all across America. There must be a way to stop this violence: how can we end the racism in our country? I don't pretend to have the answer, but it will come from within ourselves. We must treat people with respect whether they are white, black, yellow, brown, we are all equal - we are all human beings. On the night that my father was beaten, Officer Castro saw my father as a monster, someone who was up to no good because his skin color was darker than his own, and that is why he beat him. The color of our skin does not define who we are and don't let anyone tell you otherwise. I long for the day when we no longer deal with racism in America, but I am afraid that day will never come.

Our family fought against the Virginia judicial system and ultimately won. Through this experience my father and grandmother wrote *Sleep Deprivation Chamber*, a play about a man brutalized by the police who fights the case and wins. It's a story of surviving racial prejudice and discrimination. This play was performed Off-Broadway and won the Obie Award in 1996 for Best New American play. Here are some excerpts from *Sleep Deprivation Chamber.*

Act 1, Scene 3

Spotlight shines on Teddy. After dragging Teddy diagonally across this concrete drive Officer Holzer slams Teddy's face down in the ground. Teddy lands on the dirt and the wet leaves, his head just inches away from smashing into a cluster of large rocks. Officer Holzer pulls Teddy's right arm upward and kicks him several more times in his chest and then places the handcuffs on him. Another officer appears and helps Officer Holzer pull Teddy up.

David Alexander follows David Jr. out of the house and stands in the front yard. The officers place Teddy spread eagle, his upper body placed flat on the car, his face turned sideways, his legs spread wide open; he is on top of the front of a police car. Two more officers surround Teddy pinning him down on the hood of the car Teddy is dazed and can barely breathe.

Teddy: Why am I being arrested? What is the charge?

David Alexander: You can't arrest him without a charge! What's the charge? Will someone answer me? What's the charge?

Teddy: What have I done?

David Alexander: Who's in charge here? What's your name? I'm talking to you.

(Officer Holzer pays very little attention to David Alexander.)

David Alexander: What's your name? What's your name and what's the charge?

Officer Holzer: You will be told at the station.

David Alexander: At the station? I want to know now, don't you have to tell somebody why you are arresting him?

Officer Holzer: I told him.

Teddy: You never told me. Why am I being arrested?

David Alexander: Why is he being arrested?

Officer Holzer: If there's a problem you can talk to the night supervisor.

(Teddy is placed into the patty wagon.)

David Alexander: I will. David Junior, do you have a pen and paper? What's your name and badge number?

Officer Holzer: It's right here on my uniform can't you see it?

David Alexander: It's dark and you keep moving around. What is it? (He tries to read the officer's badge.) ... Holzer 892462... You have made a very big mistake, my friend. You have tangled with the wrong family. You're going to be very sorry.

Adam P. Kennedy and Joe Kennedy

Top left, Adam and Canaan in front of Adrienne's Mural at the Signature Theatre New York, 2015. Middle right, January 4, 1964 at Fredrick Eberstadt Studio, New York City, Adrienne Kennedy in Opening Night Dress for *Funnyhouse of a Negro.*

Chapter II
Adrienne Kennedy

My grandmother, Adrienne Kennedy was born in Pittsburgh, Pennsylvania but grew up in Cleveland, Ohio. Her mother, Etta Hawkins, was a was an elementary school teacher. And a graduate of Atlanta University and her father, Cornell Wallace Hawkins, a graduate of Morehouse College. and later the head of the Cedar Branch YMCA in Cleveland Ohio. She had one younger brother Cornell. The elementary school she attended was 60% white and 40% black. She would often tell me a story of a boy named Charles Wetesnik. Charles was a short white child who was not well liked, rarely speaking to anyone. One day in the 5th grade, my grandmother, as school president, was told by a group of students that Charles was being beaten up by Rosalie Miller. She was a black girl, tall in stature with broad shoulders. The students asked her to help Charles. She went over to the iron fence where

Rosalie was repeatedly kicking and striking Charles and tried to pull her off of him. When she asked Rosalie why she was beating him up she answered, "He called me a nigger." Adrienne finally got Rosalie to stop hitting him and they went their separate ways. Charles never called Rosalie a nigger again.

After the incident my grandmother was approached by a group of black students and they said, "You're a white people lover," and "You love whites." She thought she was doing the right thing to help this kid who was being beaten up, but being black and helping a white kid that no one liked made other black people dislike her.

My grandmother would often come home from school and spend her time reading and listening to her mother tell stories of when she was a child and the experiences she had to go through. Her mother, who I called Nana, was born in a small town in Georgia. She was a mulatto. Her father was white and her mother black. Like me she was fair skinned. Being half black she had to try extremely hard to make people accept her. Through the years she would often answer Adrienne's questions of racism plain and simply, "White people don't like us." This was something that stuck with my grandmother throughout her life. She had to learn to accept that white people didn't like blacks.

After graduating from high school in 1949, my grandmother attended the recently integrated Ohio State University. The blacks students couldn't go into restaurants around the campus and there was little interaction between blacks and whites. She stayed in a dorm with about six hundred girls, only thirteen who were black. Most of the girls in her dorm were from small towns in southern Ohio. They felt superior to Adrienne and all blacks, believing that blacks were an inferior race.

It wasn't just the students at Ohio State who had this attitude. Many professors didn't think blacks could perform on the same level as the white students. In an English class during her freshman year my grandmother was questioned about an essay she had written and turned into the professor the prior day. The professor said her work was outstanding but proceeded to accusingly ask , "Who wrote this?". Her professor thought she had stolen the work from a white student. The idea that blacks were inferior to the whites seemed to be a common perception among white Americans.

They showed this attitude in the way they would talk and interact with blacks. The white girls in her dorm would ridicule Adrienne and speak to her in a demeaning manner. This racial hatred towards her was something that she hadn't truly experienced before and being alone at OSU was a difficult task. She often had thoughts to transferring to another school because she couldn't stand being at Ohio State any longer.

After a semester of this environment she returned to Cleveland for Christmas break. She explained to her mother and father her hatred of the school and that she wanted to leave Ohio State. Her mother told her she was acting ridiculous and to "Not let those white people get you down." Adrienne's being at Ohio State was a sort of status symbol for her mother. She always told her friends and co-workers she wouldn't let Adrienne leave Ohio State. Ultimately she convinced Adrienne to stick it out and get her degree.

In her sophomore year she met my grandfather, Joseph Kennedy Sr., who helped her cope with the environment of Ohio State. Being with her new boyfriend made her life more bearable but in her junior year Joe headed to Columbia University to start working towards his PhD. She was alone again on this huge campus filled with white people who despised her. It was not a happy time in her life. The only white person who was kind to her was a girl named Barbara Cole. They became friends during her senior year.

Adrienne graduated from Ohio State and married Joe in 1953, and they moved to New York City. Joe worked on his PhD at Columbia. Then he received his doctoral degree in Social Psychology and got a teaching job at Hunter College. My grandfather, while working as a professor at Hunter College in 1960 received a grant for $20,000 from the African Research Foundation to conduct research in Ghana, Nigeria and Liberia. This undertaking would involve extensive travel and require that he'd be away from America for quite a long time. He decided he would take his wife and their six year old son, Joseph C. Kennedy II, with him. They boarded the ocean liner the Queen Mary in September of 1960.

Here is an excerpt from my interview with Adrienne Kennedy explaining how her trip to Africa not only changed her, but how it impacted her writing to ultimately lead to a breakthrough for her professionally and creatively. This interview was conducted on August 31, 2014 at Canaan Kennedy's home in Williamsburg, Virginia.

Adrienne Kennedy: We went to Africa in September, 1960. I had been writing a very long time. Constantly. I had a literary agent at a very well known literary agency that was called Music Corporation of America. The agent had been trying to get a couple of my stories and a novel published. But he couldn't get them published.

Canaan: At this time, did you have any works published at all?

Adrienne Kennedy: Nothing; zero. Two or three people tried to help me get them published, my teacher at Columbia and my teacher at the New School.

Adrienne: I was 29 when we got on the ship. You remember the movie now, right? *The Voyage.*[The movie she refers to is the film of the trip shot by my grandfather. It starts on the ship and ends in Liberia with the first drive from the Monrovia airport.]

Canaan: On the Queen Mary?

Adrienne Kennedy: Yes. Remember that movie? Okay, see, it's all there in the movie. In fact, you might want to use a couple of photos from the movie, because that's a beautiful movie. And that's the only thing that has survived. Joe had several movies of that trip, but that's the only one that survived.

I'll try and make it succinct. The trip, starting with the Queen Mary, London, Paris, Casablanca, Abidjan, [capital of the Ivory Coast] it took three weeks, a little bit more. Then we arrived in Liberia. We were there about a month, and then we arrived in Ghana. Then I was in Ghana basically until the end of February. I was in Africa five months.

Something happened to my mind. I had been writing all this time. People said my writing was, promising, etc. Something happened and I think it's quite accurate. It happens to a lot of people. There was something about the sun. The sun is so very intense. The moon, the moon feels like it's right there. You walk outside at night. I felt like I could just go there ...

Canaan: And grab it?

Adrienne Kennedy: And grab it, that's right. Because there is something about the landscape. I've told you that, something about the equator. I don't know. There's something about the moon, the sun, the heat, the flowers, the color of the landscape, the red soil. It's like Georgia, the red soil, the fields of green and all those exotic trees. That picture, that famous picture of Joe walking through the frangipani trees, the landscape, everything it just did something to me.

We ended up living in the Achimota Inn. The town of

Achimota is outside of Accra, Ghana. The Achimota School is very famous and the Achimota University is nearby. Kwame Nkrumah and John Atta Mills were educated at the Achimota School. Joe left the inn every morning at five am and came back about midnight. He was interviewing people. He went deep into the bush. I stayed in the inn with Joedy [Joseph Kennedy, II, my uncle] and took him to school. The Achimota School was across the green. Then I came back to the inn. There was a lot of solitude. That is very important.

Our rooms were on the second floor of the inn. It was a pretty white stucco building set in a bower of trees and had once been a rest stop for British travelers. Now it was open to everyone. Joedy had a room. Our room was the kind of room I had never seen before. It was a large room, white walls, dark green shutters and huge dark bed. The bed was totally covered in a gigantic mosquito netting. Have you ever seen that in a movie?

Canaan: No, but I have heard of mosquito netting.

Adrienne Kennedy: The whole bed from the floor to the ceiling was covered in this giant netting.
You feel like you are in a tomb. It always made me feel frightened. You have to climb in. To get into the bed you have to pull up the netting. You are covered at night, covered in this gigantic mosquito netting. And it is heavy. The mosquito netting, then the dark shutters. You never opened the shutters or the

windows. You kept the shutters closed. It made for a cool room but it was eerie. I am almost sure it had a ceiling fan. I was there alone. I sat at a little dark table and wrote. I think I picked Joedy up around one from school and we had lunch at the dining room next door to the inn. Then we went for a walk. It was very hot. There were many perfumed flowers. I had never been alone that much. And I had never been so close to the moon and the sun.

Ghana was basically all black people; of course there were loads and loads of Europeans still there. But I was in a black country. So it affected me tremendously and my writing changed. Sitting in the Achimota Inn I started to write passages of *Funnyhouse of A Negro*. Even I recognized that the passages were superior. The writing was superior to the writing I had been doing all those years. I could just tell. It had a rhythm. It had an intensity. It had a passion. I would just sit there and write. The inn had it's own servants. The servants would bring tea. It was hot. I stayed indoors except to walk to the school. I have forgotten what the temperature was. But I only walked out in the sun to get Joedy. We walked in the sun briefly. It was too hot to walk a distance. Then we would come back to the inn. I couldn't stop thinking of everything I had seen, all the history I had seen.

Remember I had never been on the Queen Mary before. I had never been on an ocean liner. I had never seen Buckingham Palace. I had never seen Versailles. I had never seen Paris, Tuilerie Gardens. All these famous things still swirled in my mind sitting there in the shuttered room. Our recent cities still loomed: I had never been to Casablanca, seen people dressed in Arabian garb. Seeing all these things had a much more powerful effect on me than I realized. Passages poured onto the page from my Remington typewriter that I had clung to all the way to Africa. Then suddenly Patrice Lumumba was murdered.

This was a very big thing that Patrice Lumumba had been murdered. I have shown you that picture so many times. The picture of Patrice Lumumba and Nkrumah walking together. Everybody had that picture. I had it on a little card and carried it with me. I understood the love that the people had for Patrice Lumumba. Patrice Lumumba became a character in the passages I was writing that I thought would be a play.

Patrice Lumumba and Kwame Nkrumah. From public domain national archives.

In front of Buckingham Palace there had been this gigantic statue of Queen Victoria. I could not stop thinking of it. Ghana had just been visited by Queen Elizabeth a few months before. The British presence was still very powerfully felt. So I made Queen Victoria a character.

Two years earlier Joe and I had taken one other big trip after he graduated from Columbia. We went on a month long trip to Mexico. We went on the train. When we were in Mexico we saw a castle. I think it was the first castle on that scale I had ever seen. It was a castle lived in by the Habsburgs when the Habsburgs occupied Mexico. It was called Chapultepec and had been built by a Spanish viceroy. You could tour it. I had never been in a castle before. It looked pretty much like it did when the Habsburgs lived there. I had always been interested in the Duchess of Habsburg, so I made the Duchess of Habsburg a character.

I'm not sure why I chose Jesus, but I've been fascinated by Jesus. I've always been fascinated by Jesus, and who Jesus is, the different images of Jesus. These characters just rose up in my mind. And I knew it was right. I'd been writing all those years and I knew it was right. They were real people. The heroine wasn't daydreaming about them. That's the huge, the most important thing. They were real people. The heroine, Sarah was sitting talking to Jesus. She was sitting talking to Queen Victoria. She was sitting talking to the Duchess of Habsburg, and Patrice Lumumba. I made them real people.

That was a gigantic leap in my writing. Gigantic. See, two or three years earlier I might have had the heroine daydream about Jesus. Or I might have had her daydream about the Duchess of Habsburg. It was a gigantic leap. It's probably why I still have a writing reputation to this very day. It gave the writing a certain distinction.

This young black girl, I made her a student. I made her a little younger than myself. I was already twenty nine, so I made her about twenty two. Other than that, she's just like me. She's dressed like me. There was no doubt that all through my twenties, even when I lived in New York and I had all kinds of friends, I was quite still preoccupied with what is the position of American Blacks? Who are we? Why do we have to struggle so? What is our place?

Canaan: And Rome?

AK: After five months Joe went to Nigeria and Joedy and I went to Rome. In Rome I took Joedy to the Parioli Day School. We left the Pensione Sabrina at 7:20 in the morning. The Sabrina was two blocks away from the American Embassy and a few yards away from Via Veneto. I think the bus came back to the Embassy about 3:20. He was in school all day. Again I had never been alone so much.

I was alone in Rome wandering around. See, I had so many levels. On one level I was very happy, because I am wandering around Rome. But all of these thoughts and images were swirling around in my head and had been for at least ten years. And it just all came into a focus. I finished *Funnyhouse* the week before Adam [my father] was born. He was born on August 1, 1961. I finished *Funnyhouse* around July 20. It definitely was all the turmoil and questions that had been swirling around in my head for at least ten years. There is no doubt about that.

Also, Rome had a certain kind of sunlight. Rome's light. And we were on the top floor of the apartment Via Reno and you could just walk from the living room onto the roof into this sunlight and see all of Rome. I would go out there every morning. You could just step onto the roof into this sunlight and see all of Rome. That's where I finished *Funnyhouse.*

I was ecstatic. It is like Van Gogh. People have been talking about this for years, forever. Certain sunlight has a powerful affect on your mind. I understand how when Van Gogh went out to the fields how sunlight of Arles (Arles is the largest city in France with many architectural and cultural locations, monuments and achievements), beat down on his brain.

I was so motivated. I was going to be thirty in September. It was very important to me that I finish this thing with all these characters before Adam was born.

Adrienne Kennedy looking out over Hudson River, Manhattan
New York. Photographer unknown.

Great Lakes Theatre Festival in Ohio, Featuring Adrienne
Kennedy's Play Ohio State Murders.

Ohio State Murders

My grandmother had been trying to write a play about Ohio State University for thirty years. The events and the landscape of Ohio State had always haunted my grandmother. She stated that, "Growing up in Cleveland, Ohio people were judged on their abilities not on their race." The environment at Ohio State was drastically different and made her feel like a lesser human being because most of the kids at Ohio State came from deeply segregated communities.

In the fall of 1989 my grandmother became a lecturer at Stanford, and she had been commissioned to write a play about Ohio State. She had already accepted the advance for the play and was afraid that she would have to give it back. One afternoon at Stanford University my grandmother was having lunch in her apartment after a lecture. Most of the time she would have lunch at the table in the kitchen, above this table were glass cabinets filled with china and dishes that were rarely used. On this particular day she decided to have lunch at her desk. While having lunch an earthquake shook San Francisco and the Stanford campus. In fear she ran inside a closet to hide. After the earthquake ended she exited the closet and after looking around at the damage she noticed that in the kitchen all of the glass dishes, china plates and the cabinets had been destroyed, falling right onto the table she sat at almost every day.

The earthquake was very dramatic and aftershocks shook the campus. There was quite a bit of damage to her building so she had to sleep in a different location because they taped off her apartment, they blocked it off for about two weeks. After those events she returned to New York City for Christmas break and then suddenly this play started pouring out of her. Finally she was able to write a play about Ohio State, she finished it before the new semester started in January. It was titled *Ohio State Murders*, it was her attempt to write about the racism and the hatred that she faced at Ohio State University.

My grandmother sent it to the producer at the Ohio Theatre, Mary Bill, who said she really liked it, but she suggested that the play be performed at the Carriwell Theatre which was the black theatre in Cleveland. My grandmother wanted the play to be performed on Playhouse Square at the Ohio Theater, where she saw movies and plays growing up. She got in contact with the director of the theatre and finally convinced them to have the play at the Ohio Theatre. The Ohio Theatre is famous for discovering Tom Hanks, a well renowned actor.

Preparation for the play went on and the theatre was looking for someone to play the lead, Suzanne Alexander. My grandmother had an idea in her mind to ask Ruby Dee if she wanted to play the lead. She met Ruby when she came to my grandmother's book signing of *People Who Led To My Plays* at this huge bookstore in the World Trade Center. There were four to five hundred people attending and near the end of the event she looked over to see Ruby Dee sitting at a table by herself wearing a gold blouse, looking up at her in admiration. She was absolutely stunned. Ruby said, "I love your book and I would love to write a book like that," and she said, "Ossie [Ossie Davis, her husband] and I have been trying to get our book published. It's about the people I have met. Can I send it to you?". Ruby sent to it my grandmother and it was similar to *People Who Led To My Plays*, with notes of people she met.

So having known Ruby Dee my grandmother wrote her a letter asking if she would like to be in her play and she replied back saying she would love to star in *Ohio State Murders*. Ruby came by her apartment on 89th street in New York City and they had lunch and discussed the play. My grandmother told me that she learned so much from her because she didn't act like "Ruby Dee". She was so genuine and unpretentious, and that was a key to her success.

So Ruby became the lead and it was a huge event in Cleveland. In fact it was the first time a black playwright had their work done at the Ohio Theatre. Ossie Davis came on the opening night and the black community came to support the play. The mayor of Cleveland announced that March 7th would be know as Adrienne Kennedy Day. She was honored and overwhelmed by the support her hometown gave her.

In 2003 Ohio State University honored my grandmother by awarding her with an Honorary Doctorate. Lesley Ferris, the head of the Ohio State University Theatre department coordinated everything that happened that year. The school had an entire year of her plays, putting on performances of *Ohio State Murders* and of *Sleep Deprivation Chamber* and teaching many more of her plays. She received her Honorary Doctorate with people such as business mogul Ted Turner, the founder of CNN and actor Christopher Reeves, best known for playing Superman. She was in total shock because she was being honored by this school where she faced so much torment, hatred and racism. To be recognized by this institution for her work as a writer and playwright was utterly amazing. She says that this was one of the happiest moments of her entire life, she couldn't believe that this little kid who used to get upset by these white girls, was now marching in with Robert Havener while they were playing the Ohio State anthem. The president of Ohio State gave her the diploma and that was thrilling to her because her peers at Ohio State thought she was nothing. The whole event was truly fulfilling to her.

In 2007 she was asked about what she thought of the racial attitudes chronicled in Ohio State Murders and she said, "I feel still [that] white society is disdainful of people of color. There is an underlying jealousy of these civilizations. Everything is in the light now...no more days when European ministers can sit in dark places and hatch secret plots. To me the attitude toward Iraq encapsulates all of this. Why would anyone think they are capable of going to another country and telling them how to run their affairs?"

Charles Isherwood of the New York Times wrote a column on December 23rd, 2007 titled 'Not all the News was on the Rialto,' which included an article about my grandmother, he said that she was, "An inspiring reminder that the country's great playwrights are not all white males, living or dead".

My grandmother faced, endured and then thrived over racism in America by using her experiences to fuel her writing career. Samuel French, Inc. called *Ohio State Murders* an "Unusual and chilling look at the destructiveness of racism in the United States". Here is an excerpt from the play *Ohio State Murders.*

Act 1

Suzanne: The police also suspected a neighbor of Mrs. Tyler's, but David, Aunt Louise, and Mrs. Tyler all said it had to be a stranger.

Alice, his sister, David said, was crocheting another bib; this one was pale yellow. It was spring. Two years had passed since I lived in the dorm,

David and Mrs. Tyler told me every day that all this would be resolved and that one day the police would discover who had followed me in the snow.

Right after Easter Mrs. Tyler told me a grad student from Ohio State was coming that evening. He was doing a study of Negroes in the Columbus area and had heard from campus housing that she kept students and was also a native of Columbus and knew a great deal about the depression years there and the development of the neighborhoods.

When I left she was expecting him for an interview and had made cocoa.

David had gotten me a job in the law library in the stacks. The hours were 6:00 to 9:30. By 10:00 p.m. I was home. We saved money. David worked on two part time jobs. Aunt Lou gave us something. That evening we pulled the car out of the drive at 5:20 to go to the law library. When we returned at 10:05 the Ohio State murders had occurred. Robert Hampshire (posing as a researcher) had killed Carol, our twin, and himself. It seems that once inside Mrs. Tyler's living room he told her he was the father of the twins, that he had never been able to forget their existence. They ruined his life. He said he knew that one day I would reveal this, that he would be investigated, there would be tests and his whole career would fail.

He admitted he had waited for me outside the doctor's office and had taken Cathi. He told her that he tried to follow the advice of his father who lived near London who had told him to just ignore me but he had been unable to do that. He was quite mad, she said, and had pushed her into the hallway and down the cellar stairs. When her son returned at 8:55 he found her crying and injured on the dark stairwell. Upstairs in the small sewing room where Carol and I slept Robert had killed Carol and himself (with a knife he had taken from the kitchen sink).

James Earl Jones doing a reading for the launch of the Adrienne Kennedy Season, at the Signature Theatre, New York.

Adrienne & Joseph Kennedy at Ohio State.

My grandfather and famed actor William Marshall who was othello on Broadway and starred in Blacula, picnic in upstate New York 1956.

Chapter III
Dr. Joseph Kennedy

J oseph C. Kennedy was born in 1926 and grew up in Franklin, Ohio. He attended Howard University and received his B.A and M.A degrees from Ohio State University and his PhD in Social Psychology from Columbia University. He served in the Korean War as a psychiatrist dealing with soldiers who had suffered from mental illness. My grandfather joined the Peace Corps working his way up to Peace Corps Director in Sierra Leone and then Regional Director for the East Asia and Pacific Region.

After leaving the Peace Corps he co-founded a non profit organization, *Africare* which works towards improving the lives of Africans by providing water and medical treatment, as well as setting up refugee camps and strengthening relations between American blacks and Africans, as well as setting up refugee camps and strengthening relations between American blacks and Africans. Since its formation in 1973 *Africare* has raised over two billion dollars in aid to 36 countries across Africa. Dr. Joseph Kennedy retired as Vice President in 1999 but his organization lives on working to improve lives of others.

Here are excerpts from my interview on Dr. Joseph Kennedy's time in Korea in the 1950s. Conducted on August 25, 2014 at Canaan Kennedy's home in Williamsburg, Virginia.

Dr. Kennedy: "I went to Camp Kilmer in Virginia. I went there and that's where they test you. They said, "Okay." They had this corporal interviewing me and I said, "Well I don't think that you quite know what I should do." I had a masters and I had studied reading and psychology. They said, "Okay, we'll put you down as a 1289 MOS, Military Occupational Specialist." I was with 1289, in health and medical. I went to training and finished.

One funny thing. I was an enlisted man but I had studied, like I said, psychology and rapid reading and so on. During the school breaks, or during the summer, reservists come to camp to do some military work. There was this class that I was teaching. When you enter the room they always say, "Here are your people. Attention!" Everybody has to stand up. These are captains and a couple colonels and I'm a private. "At ease," the presenting/introducing officer would say. They would sit down and then I would do my lecturing. When the class was over they say, "Well thank you, Captain Kennedy." I said, "No, I'm not a captain. I'm a private."

So I was sent to the Medical Service Corps." I said, "All right." I went and Adrienne and I had just gotten married in May. In May I was assigned to Fitzsimons

Army Hospital in Denver Colorado. It was nice because I wore my uniform during the day and after whatever time, 5:30 or so, I could take the uniform off. I didn't have to wear it. Then I had a nice apartment there with Adrienne. Nice living room and so on. I was there for about, let's see, May to December, about 4 months.

One day they called me in, they said, "Okay, Mr. Kennedy, we have a request for one 1289 MOS Negro." It turned out that there was only one other black guy with that MOS. He was away off somewhere so when they said, "One Negro," I said, "Okay. It must be special since they're calling me by name, so to speak."

We went to, I think it was, Tacoma, Washington and took the ship. It was nineteen days on the water going to Japan. I'm saying to myself, "Since they specified one Negro, that's me, I'm going to be in Tokyo." When we arrived we got on this train. The train just sped on through Tokyo and that was the end of that. It went through Nagasaki and Hiroshima beyond to Sasebo. Sasebo was the last point in Japan that led to Korea.

There in Sasebo, the question now was whether you're going to get a parka, a heavy coat, or a light coat. If you got the heavy coat, you were going north. I got the light coat. I got on the ... they called it the Pusan ferry. Pusan, if you know Korea, of course, it is the tip of Korea. North Korea had driven South Korea all the way to what they called the Pusan perimeter. That's where I ended up, Pusan. I went into the office there and the commander said, "We don't use your MOS at this level so you will be a combat medic." He said, "By the way, do you know how to type?" I said, "I know how to type." They said, "Okay, you'll become the typist for all of our records and so on, and the news that we put out."

That was my first assignment but I still had to walk sentry with my rifle. Then, once or twice a week, I don't remember why, but I had to go to this house, like a little house or tent, and I had to be there to protect it. I would go there and I would spend the night there.

In Pusan, this now is in January and it's cold. It was so cold. You'd go to the washroom, bathroom, and you had to chip the ice to get your water. It was just that cold. It was freezing cold. If you wanted to go to urinate, they had, right outside the tent, there was a pipe. It went down into the ground and that's where you urinated. If you had to do a number two, then you had to go to the toilet. The toilet was down a little hill. It was cold. It was just freezing, freezing cold.

I don't know how long I was there. The captain of the outfit, he disappeared for a couple days and we were always saying, "Oh, is he going to Tokyo?" We would all go to Tokyo. He came back and he was angry and he said he was going north.

We went from Pusan ... now by this time fighting had stopped and there was the demilitarized line. He said, "We're going north." We got on the train and we went all the way up to the demilitarized line. It was a place called Yango Valley. It was right there at the demilitarized line. There I was. I was a combat medic. The fighting had ended but I was there. I didn't do much. I had a detachment with two other people, so there were three of us in this tent. One day we had a patient and had to take him to Seoul. I asked if I could assist in taking the patient to Seoul. Seoul was the capital. When I got to Seoul. I went to the medical division. It's a place like, did you ever see the movie *M*A*S*H?*

Canaan: No I never saw it. Is it like a headquarters?

Dr. Kennedy: It's a hospital for the wounded and sick. I went there and I said, "Do you have a need for someone with this background, a psychology background?" They said, "Well as a matter of fact we do." I said, "Okay, will you contact the people up there in Yango Valley and tell them that you're going to accept me here in Seoul?" I went to Seoul and that's where I was assigned to the military hospital, as in *M*A*S*H,* where the wounded and the neurotic and the psychotic patients were. There were two separate, like, huge tents. We had the neurotic, they were just there. Like this one fellow, he said, "I just didn't want to fight anymore. I refused to fight." They said, "What do you do with him?" They sent him to this hospital. He was in the neurotic section.

Then the psychotics were those who could be violent. We had to strap them all down. In the psychotic division these patients were strapped. In the neurotic, they were just there. In testing the psychotic, I don't know if you know the Rorschach test; you know the Rorschach inkblot? You have these inkblots and then you interpret.

Canaan: You show the patient and they have to say what they think it is.

Dr. Kennedy: Right. This one guy, I showed him the inkblot, "What do you see?" "Oh, a pretty lady." Showed him the next inkblot, "What do you see?" "A pretty lady." Another inkblot, all he saw was a pretty lady. The officer said, "Is that all you see? Do you see anything else?" When they came, they all hoped that they would be evacuated and go to Tokyo, but instead they went back to the service, back to their units.

Then there was this fellow, I think there were about four of us doing the testing. I heard one of my companions, he came and he said, "This black guy, he's saying that people are writing about him back home in magazines and so on and we think he's psychotic." I said, "What's his name?" They said "Ray Price." He was a black singer and *Jet Magazine* had been writing articles about him. When they told me his name I started laughing. I said, "Well he's not psychotic, he's telling you the truth. They are writing about him."

Canaan: That's funny. What happens to most of these people?

Dr. Kennedy: Who were strapped in?

Canaan: Yes.

Dr. Kennedy: They stayed strapped in.

Canaan: Did they end up going to mental hospitals when they got back?

Dr. Kennedy: Well, no. I don't know what happened to them. Like I say, there were some in the psychotic that got strapped down and that was that.

Canaan: Okay.

Dr. Kennedy: At this camp now, this is in Seoul, and the camp is on the outskirts, a place called Chun Jung Ni, I'll never forget that. That's where our camp was. On the weekends they would have the officer's club and the enlisted men's club. I'm an enlisted man, I was a private, or a corporal by that time. The enlisted men had to go to the enlisted men's place. We'd have, on Friday's, we'd have music and some dancing. In the morning we would go back to Seoul and that was that."

Canaan: Thank you. Tell me about life at Columbia University?

Dr. Kennedy: When I first started at Columbia, Adrienne and I, we weren't married. I went to Columbia, I was staying on the campus. Let's see, now. I was staying on the campus. I had a job. I worked at the post office. I had to be on the job at 11:00 at night and leave at 7:00 in the morning. Sometimes I didn't have a class. I'd go home and sleep and would have to get up around 9:00 in the evening to go to the post office.

A number of times, several days, I would have a quick bite to eat and I would go to class. I remember this class, for some reason I sat in the front row and I'd always go to sleep. Sitting there just sleeping, sleeping. I had these classes and I had the top, best known social psychologist in the world, Otto Klineberg, and he was my professor. I did my dissertation and I did research. I went to Morgan, Hampton and Howard and interviewed students. These are all black colleges. I interviewed them on the stereotypes. I had about eighty questions I would ask them. Like, who do you think is the smartest? Who will achieve?

Canaan: The people in your classroom were all white? Were you the only black?

Dr. Kennedy: Yes, I was the only black.

Canaan: Out of how many people would you say, were in your class?

Dr. Kennedy: This is higher level graduate school so probably about fifteen of us in the class. Then, at some point, we had to actually teach one class.

Canaan: Did they have any particular attitude towards you? Did they not like you?

Dr. Kennedy: No, no, no. These are graduate students . We were all there on some equal level.

Canaan: All right.

Dr. Kennedy: Then I had to go to defend my thesis and this one professor, a lady, she criticized something about my research. She said I would have to correct it. This was like on a Monday. Now I had to have my thesis in by Friday in order to graduate. This was Monday and she said I had to make these changes. She knew I was finished but I went and stayed up all night and on Wednesday I went in with the changes and they accepted it. She said, "I've never known anyone who persevered as much as you do. I've never known anybody who could persevere like that and overcome." I got my doctorate. Mama was there, Uncle James, brother James and Adrienne and Joedy. They were there for the graduation. That was Columbia.

Canaan: At Columbia, was there any racial tension?

Dr. Kennedy: No.

Canaan: Anything?

Dr. Kennedy: No, well, again, I had two roommates. One was from Nicaragua and the other was from Brooklyn and was Jewish. No, there were two roommates, we got along fine. No problem. No problem at all. You had to pass a test in order to enter the doctoral program at that level. You had to pass this test. I passed that test and that's how I got into the doctoral program. No, at Columbia there was no sign of prejudice.

Canaan: At Ohio State, were there any racial tensions that you experienced?

Dr. Kennedy: It was terrible. Ohio State was terrible because, first of all, right across the street from the campus there were a couple of restaurants. Blacks couldn't go in there. A couple of us would go in there and they wouldn't serve us and we would sue them and get a few dollars. That was right across the street from the campus. Then there was an old student union and the blacks would go there.

There was a lot of prejudice. As a matter of fact, I went out for football. I weighed 170 pounds and, of course, at Ohio State they had, maybe, 100 people trying out. I was on the fourth team. One day the fourth team played the first team and this guy, who was a fullback, he must have weighed at least 235 pounds, he came roaring through and I tackled him, knocked him down. He got up, I didn't get up. My shoulder was dislocated so that was the end of that. Blacks could play football and track. Couldn't play basketball. Again, that was the time the basketball was all black and all white. You didn't have ...

Canaan: Mixing.

Dr. Kennedy: You couldn't.

Canaan: Do you remember any type of attitudes people had towards you when talking to you?

Dr. Kennedy: No. Well, not really, because, as I said, we didn't really intermingle.

Canaan: The few black people that were at Ohio State would stick together and the white people would stick together?

Dr. Kennedy: Right. When we'd go to the student union, like I said, the whites are over here, the blacks are over there. There's really no real interaction. That was especially true when we were getting ready to go to the football games. We'd go to the student union and then go to the football game.

Canaan: At the football games, the blacks would sit in one section, whites would sit in the rest?

Dr. Kennedy: No, no, no. In the stadium, you're talking about, at that time, eighty, ninety thousand people. There was no discrimination in the stadium.
Canaan: Okay.

Dr. Kennedy: That wasn't a problem. Again, no basketball and no swimming.

Canaan: Were there any teachers that you had any difficult situations with?

Dr. Kennedy: No. I was a good student. I had three roommates and we were off campus. This one fellow, he would stay up all night, presumably studying, and then when we'd go to the campus, and again, this is a huge campus. We'd get there eight, nine in the morning and we'd each go our different ways and different classes so we wouldn't see each other. We had a fraternity, a black fraternity. White fraternities, white sororities and black sororities. With the black fraternity, we registered. We had to register in this overall umbrella for fraternities, that's when I discovered that two of my roommates weren't even in school. They weren't in school. Every morning they'd leave as if they were going to class. As I told you, the campus was so big you'd go off so I didn't know where you went. You were studying something, you go over there. I'm studying something, over there.
We would get to the school, go to class, they'd head off. We were roommates. As I said, this one guy would get up and pretend to study. Then I found out that he and that other roommate weren't even in school, and their two girlfriends, they weren't in school either. The four of them, they were just there living it up but they weren't taking any classes.

Canaan: That's funny.
Dr. Kennedy: Ohio State was just segregated. I remember when I first went from Howard to Ohio State there was a white girl in my class, and somehow

we talked. Then we would go out, people would lay out on the grass on the campus. I would lay out there with this white girl. People looked but no problems. That was a nice relationship.

Ohio State was huge and there was the memories of Jesse Owens and one of his daughters, Gloria, went to Ohio State at that time. No, whites and blacks just didn't go places together or work out together, even the gyms were segregated.

Dr. Joseph Kennedy & Nelson Mandela, 1994.

Dr. Kennedy getting directions in Ghana.

Journey to Africa

In 1994 my grandfather, Dr. Joseph Kennedy wrote his autobiography, *Color in a Cage,* here is an excerpt where he reflects on the attitude people had towards Africa.

"Perhaps the greatest awareness of color came when the white boys and girls would yell at me, after calling me nigger - 'Hey, let me see your tail. Hey black monkey go back to Africa where you came from and swing in the trees.'[Circa late 1930s, early 1940s] Maybe I began to believe the saying 'If you're white you're alright, if you're brown stick around, but if you're black get back.'"

To be black was to be inferior. My classmates told me that and all around me, my environment - the school books, magazines which showed Colored people only as butlers holding a tray of whiskey or a ham, or Colored women only as mammy-maids - cried out that what they said was true. The movies proclaimed it to be true and only occasionally was there a Colored "featured" singer.

I was told - 'Go back to Africa where you came from. Africa is jungles and monkeys and cannibals. You come from nothing, you are nothing, and you will be nothing.'

At home, my mother and father would gather us, the six children, around the table and read stories of ancient Abyssinia, of the Kingdom of Ethiopia. They read about the glories of Egypt, and in that home I knew I came from Africa, and I knew I came from a glorious Africa; an Africa that had been, that was, that would be."

Dr. Kennedy and Joe Kennedy in Ghana.

Canaan: How did you get the grant from the African Research Foundation?

Dr. Kennedy: I had finished my doctorate and I started teaching at Hunter College. I have told you that when we were growing up we would all sit around this large table, all six children and have a prayer. Every child had to have a bible verse. I always laughed. My sister Irene always said "Jesus wept." Our parents read to us about Africa. And it became my dream to go to Africa.

I have told you about my professor, Otto Klineberg. He was invited to teach at the University of Ghana. He also had an offer to go to Brazil to study how Brazil had freed their slaves, and how it was different from how slaves had been freed in the United States. In Brazil, if you were born in Brazil you were free. That was unlike the United States. I wanted to go to Ghana. I had an opportunity through Otto Klineberg, but he was contesting the leadership of Kwame Nkrumah and he had to leave Ghana. That was the end of that opportunity.

I said, "Okay, I'm going to go and look in the telephone directory." This was 1960. "I'm going to go and look in the telephone directory and any place that has Africa in the name I'm going to call them." I called the African Research Foundation. I called them and I talked with this fellow, James Monroe. I always remember that, James Monroe, and I talked to him and he had another foundation called the Human Ecology Fund. So we talked on the phone and he said, "Come in." I went in and we talked and he said, "Okay, I'll give you a grant."

Then a couple of days later I got a call from him and he said three psychologists on the team told him they didn't get any references. So then I went to Otto Klineberg, the preeminent psychologist. A few days later I got a call to come in and they were so impressed because Otto Klineberg had sent a handwritten recommendation for me so that's how I got the grant, and it was to go to Liberia, Ghana, and Nigeria.

I was going to do a takeoff of what I'd done for my doctorate which was stereotypes and so on; it was called "Emerging African Images", and so that was going to be my research. They gave me a grant and next thing I knew Adrienne and Joedy, I guess he was about six years old, we were on the Queen Mary heading off to Europe.

We flew from Madrid to Liberia. When we got to Liberia there were no buses or anything going into the capital so I got in this taxi, some rickety taxi. The driver sped down the dusty dirt roads. People were walking in the road and they just seemed to ignore the car. And then, at the last minute, they'd jump over into a ditch and the car kept speeding. When we got to the hotel in Monrovia the taxi driver said the price would be so and so. Don't remember exact figure but I knew it was too much. I didn't know how much it should be but I definitely knew it was too much. I said, "That is too much. I can't pay that." That is when I first came in contact with African bargaining. You never accept the first offer because they start up. And then you go down. The hotel was the St. George's and the proprietor was St. George himself. The little room had bugs, beetles and mosquitoes. I knew no one in Liberia. I knew no one in Africa. It was just Adrienne, Joedy and I.

There was a black American at the YMCA and I went to him. He said, "What is St. George charging you?" I told him and he said "Okay". He went with me to the St. George and said to St. George, "You are charging him too much."   George said, "I didn't know they were friends of yours." He reduced the price but it was a terrible room, bugs everywhere.

There was only one decent restaurant. So we went there. It was three dollars a person, for the three of us, nine dollars. For breakfast, lunch and dinner, that is twenty seven dollars. I could not afford it. So I said. "Adrienne, let's get out of here."

I knew the whole history of Liberia. Liberia had been settled by slaves who returned there from America. I knew how astounding Liberia had been in withstanding the invasion of the European colonization. But at that time I was not impressed with Liberia. We stayed about one month then flew to Ghana.

We went to Accra in Ghana and stayed at this very fine hotel, the Ambassador; very famous and historic. It was too expensive to stay there long term so we stayed in their cottages. Every morning a bus would come and take us to the hotel for breakfast, fabulous hotel, but we would go there and sit down and I would say to the waiter "Bring us some coffee first." Now in the European tradition you drink coffee after you eat. But I still said, "Bring us some coffee." No coffee. Then we would order. We would eat, finish, then he would bring coffee. I said, ok, I know what I'll do. The next day we went into the dining room and he said, "What would you like to eat?" I told him we wouldn't be eating. Just bring us some coffee. He'd bring us coffee and then I said, "We have changed our minds. We do want to eat." We did that a number of times and I guess he never caught on or maybe he thought this dumb American.

Then there was Professor St. Clair Drake there who was great. He was from Chicago and was teaching at the University of Legon. He was a famous sociologist and anthropologist. He knew Nkrumah. So I met Nkrumah. Ghana was just fantastic. It was independent. Freedom was sweeping Africa. In two years there were fifteen African countries that became independent. Ghana was first in 1957. Going out in the mornings, driving on the road, dusty roads, people waving, children smiling. It was just fabulous.

Canaan: What were you doing specifically?

Dr Kennedy: I wanted to find out what Africans, what Ghanaians thought of Liberia and Ghana and Nigeria and what they thought of the Europeans, of the French and the British because they had been the top colonizers, and about black Americans. And so that was the research and again I called it "Emerging African Images". So we would travel going into the villages, way up north where people ran naked. We had this little Volkswagen, a Beetle and in those days the Beetle didn't have a gas meter. There was no meter so you had to be very careful considering gas and how far you were traveling. Up north they've never seen an outsider, an American black, only white missionaries. When they saw me they hid from me. That was one place they would call me "Oburoni,

Oburoni".

When I arrived in Ghana they had just had a census so
I had access to the whole census, about eight million
people, and that's how I organized my visits around
the country. Harry Welbeck, a young student was now
working with me. I asked him, "What does Oburoni
mean?" He said, "It means white man." I sat down
with this Ghanaian Chief and I said, (I put my hand
out) "We're the same color. What kind of man are
you?" He said, " I am a black man." "What about
me?", I said. "You're a white man." I said, "What do
you mean?" And again he said, "You're a white man."
Then later I understood. See, I came in a white man's
car. I spoke the white man's language, so I had to be
white. It wasn't color. It was the customs.

We'd go into this village. There was a chief. He had
thirty wives. A man could have as many wives as you
could support. He had thirty and this huge compound
and a little house for each of his wives. We went into
this huge compound. He was there on his throne.
Naked children sat on his side. He poured a libation.
We had palm wine. The chief would drink some, pass
it to the next person who would then pass it to me and
you do that several times. It was just fantastic.
Fantastic.

It was just wonderful being in Ghana and meeting
Nkrumah. There was this big statue of him in
downtown Accra. To see the big statue of the man and
then to meet him. It was unbelievable. We were up in

the country and it was very quiet. Nkrumah said, "Lumumba has just been killed in the Congo." And it was quiet even in the city. It was quiet; even the drums stopped playing. Now the drums, they had talking drums, these big drums and they would send out messages on them - say they wanted to have a meeting and wanted people to come. Everybody now has cell phones. Ghana was just fantastic.

Then I went to Nigeria. And then I went to Ibadan which is up country from Lagos. The university is in Ibadan. I went there and this professor said, "We will give you an office." Immediately I had an office but no place to live. Adrienne and Joedy had gone to Rome. I was there by myself in Nigeria. He said, "We will find a place for you but in the meantime you can stay in the student dormitory." So for about two weeks I was in the dormitory with the Nigerian students. Then I got this very nice apartment. Nigeria was so big. I had to get people from different sections of the country to help me. Most of the time in most of these places maybe just one person could speak English and that would be a teacher. At Ibadan they would hire people to help me with the research. Then to escape Ibadan I would drive to Lagos. Often I drove to Lagos. There was this nice hotel. I told them I wanted to go to a club not where expatriates went but where Nigerians went. The porter at the hotel said "Okay, you go the Coo-ka-ten." I said, "Okay." So I get in a taxi, "I want to go to Coo-ka-ten." Over a period of a month I went to the Coo-ka-ten. Finally I said to somebody. "What is a Coo-ka-ten? What is that?" They said, "It is a 'Cool Cats Inn'." All that time I had been calling it "Coo-ka-ten." And it was the "Cool Cats Inn".

Nigeria at that time was peaceful and it was wonderful to go from Ibadan down to Lagos. Really nice. It was a free country.

I finished my research in Nigeria. Then I went to Rome. Adrienne and Joedy were there and it is where Adam was born. I arrived in Rome on Saturday morning. All day Saturday and Sunday we walked around Rome. Sunday night we went to a movie. When we came out Adrienne said she was in labor. We rushed to the hospital Salvator Mundi. Adam was born at 3:30 in the morning August 1. I remember I bought a white basket to put him in, a little white basket. We were in Rome six more weeks then left for LeHavre to board the ship back to the America. We carried the little white basket to the ship. As we approached the ship *The United States* and I asked Joedy for the tickets. I had given him the tickets to carry on the train from Paris to LeHavre. We were approaching the ship and I said "Joedy give me the tickets." He had lost the tickets. We walked back the way we came and fortunately the tickets were on the ground. So we got on the ship and sailed to New York. We had been gone exactly one year.

I came back to New York. It was the end of September. We lived in the Park West Village, a brand new complex on 100th street and Central Park

West in a beautiful spacious apartment.

Very soon after I wrote an article on "Emerging African Images", my research. And it was published in the *New York Times Magazine* section. "American Negroes Key Role in Africa", that was the title. And out of that I was on way. That launched me. I was still working with the outfit that sent me to Africa. One day the director called me into his office. He said, "How would you like to go to the Soviet Union?" There is this group called Promoting Enduring Peace. This was 1962. He said, "For about three years the group has wanted Americans to join. They are reading about and hearing about the Civil Rights Movement but have never seen any black Americans. They want us to join them." He asked would I go? So I went to Russia with Promoting Enduring Peace. I spent seven weeks in the Soviet Union. That was the result of the *New York Times* article.

On each floor there was an attendant that would check you out. Russia had started bringing in Africans to study in Russia. I wanted to interview them. They were at this huge hotel. I got a taxi. The taxi driver said, "Don't get out of the taxi in front of the hotel or leave the hotel in a taxi. All the people out in front work for the government. They are Secret Service." So when I left the interview I walked down the street and then got a taxi. There was a university in Russia named after Patrice Lumumba. I decided to go there. A lady at the door told me I didn't have a permit but since I was there she let me in. So I interviewed

African students. I wrote an article "African Students In Russia" It was published there. I have a copy somewhere. So that was the Soviet Union.

Dr. Joseph Kennedy in Russia.

I continued to work for the American Society For Africa. Then I went to the Peace Corps and was interviewed by many different people. They said "How would you like to be the Deputy for the Research Division?" I said, "Who is the director?" "We do not have a director." I said, "Well, why don't you make me the director?" "No, no." I said, "Okay, goodbye." So that was it with the Peace Corps. Then about two years later, I went back and that's when I met with the Deputy Director for the African region and I told him, "I'd like to go to Sierra Leone," and that's how I became Peace Corps Director to Sierra Leone. After that I came back and he made me

Director of the East Asia and Pacific region. At the time no black had held that position.

Canaan: The director of what?

Dr. Kennedy: East Asia and the Pacific region. East Asia was South Korea, Philippines, Malaysia, and the islands of the South Pacific, Samoa, Fiji, Tonga and Micronesia. I was in charge of that region. One of my first meetings, one of the people who was now working under me said, "They don't like black people out there." [in his region.] I said, "When I first went to Africa, I was told that the Africans didn't like black Americans out there." I said, "I proved that to be wrong and I will prove this to be wrong." And I did.

Canaan: Tell me about the creation of *Africare*.

Dr. Kennedy: In 1971 I got a call from C. Payne Lucas. He was at Peace Corps. He was on like the 5th floor or something. He said, "Come down to my office." So I went down and he said he had had this request through Oumarou Youssoufou, from the President of Niger [Hamani Diori] to see if he could do something about this organization called *Africare,* started by Bill Kirker. While he was great at getting people to come as volunteers - he had about 17 volunteers - he wasn't a good administrator so they were leaving Niger. President Diori asked Luke if he could get involved and do something about this organization. That's when Luke called me and we talked.
In May of 1971, C. Payne Lucas, Bill Kirker, Al

Alemian and myself, the four of us and, of course, Oumarou over there in Niger sat down and reconstituted Africare. Kirker had it as a volunteer organization. The problem was that he hadn't figured what to do if a volunteer got sick, had to be evacuated and so on. So that's where the lack of administration part came in. We incorporated it in 1971 with the twofold goal of improving the quality of life in Africa, especially in the areas of agriculture, water, health, and refugee assistance. The second goal was to increase the interaction between Africans and Americans of African descent. Those were the two goals.

So Kirker went back to Africa with his volunteers, Kevin and Al went off, and Luke and I were there [in Washington, DC]. Not much was happening. We were trying to raise money. Then President Diori came to a meeting in Canada, I think in Montreal. So Luke and I went to Montreal on our own money and met with Oumarou and President Diori. That's what we call the first board meeting of *Africare*. So it was held in Montreal, Canada. I guess that was 1972.

The ambassador from Niger, unfortunately I don't remember his name, but because he was a tremendous supporter of *Africare*, the Niger ambassador gave us a small office in the Niger embassy. So there we were, but not much was happening.

Then Luke had the idea to kick off Africare in Atlanta. We chose Atlanta for a number of reasons. I've forgotten the family's name, but it was a black family in Atlanta that several years earlier had started a for-profit company that took people to Africa. Then there were several other people there. Of course, by that time Andy Young had been a Congressman, so there were some connections there.

So we officially launched Africare in 1972 in Atlanta, Georgia. Andy Young and Coretta King, they were there. We got a letter from then Governor Jimmy Carter. That was the highlight at that point, going to Atlanta and launching there.

Then around November of 1972, we got a grant from AID [The United States Agency for International Development]. The AID administrator was a black lady named Golar Butcher. She was the Director of the African bureau of AID. She gave us a grant, a $100,000 grant to do a feasibility study in Difa [Niger], and that's where Kirker had worked at the hospital. Of course, he was still there, he had gone back there. So we got that grant.

Then Diori, and again, this is through Oumarou, said 'There's this drought in Niger and throughout the Sahel and no one is saying anything at all about it. Why don't you, *Africare*, say something." That was in 1973. So we started talking about the drought in the Sahel. We lined up about twenty families in Washington, DC, all black, and asked them to host a reception. Each one would host their own reception to raise some money for the drought in the Sahel.
That's what we did. It was very successful. Luke and

I scampered around Washington trying to go to every one of them. It was very successful. We raised $60,000 starting from the first of the year through, I guess July or something. We raised about $60,000. Sam Stokes, he had been a Peace Corp volunteer, he and I went to Africa to give this $60,000 to the six heads of state. So we had like $10,000 for each of the countries. Sam Stokes and I went, and there was this huge conference for the formation of the ... I think it was called something like the European Fund for the Sahel. It was an organization bringing together nations, various countries, in Europe and the United States. They were meeting in Niamey [Niger], so that's where Sam Stokes and I went to deliver the $60,000. We decided that I was going to take this money with Sam Stokes. Let me finish this and I'll back up. President Nixon had requested that Diori invite the U.S, not the ambassador but the head of the AID to this conference, and Diori turned him down. So the U.S. representation was not there.

Sam Stokes and I sat there with Oumarou through this conference, and it went on for three or four days. There were like 100 people there or something. We were thinking to ourselves that they had forgotten about us. On the last day of the conference Oumarou told us that there was a last reception at the President's palace for all of the conferees, and Sam and I were invited, and that's where we would give them the money.

We went to this reception, it was out in the garden.

There was this huge room. In order to get to the garden, you had to pass this room. There we were in the garden, Sam Stokes and I, with these six heads of state. They were from Mali, Senegal, Upper Volta, Niger, Chad and Mauritania.

We met with the six heads of state, and I didn't know a word of French, so Sam translated. I gave this check to [President Leopold Sengor of Senegal] Sengor and he accepted it and made some remarks. Then, through Sam, I said, "Mr. President. Mr. President, I must take the check back, because it is a $60,000 check, but it is $10,000 for each country, so I must take the check back." They all laughed. But the point is that we were visible when everybody was coming out to the garden they saw us, these Americans, though Nixon had been turned down. There we were giving this $60,000.

Then we got former Peace Corps volunteers who had served in each of those countries, so they knew something about the country. Each one of them, we gave them the $10,000 here in the United States and we paid their way there. They didn't get paid any salary; it was all volunteer. Each one of them had the $10,000 to decide how to distribute it and what to do with it in each country.

Some time during this period of the drought, before we went to Africa, Sam and I - Luke was in Diffa [Niger]. I went on television with this black lady. Unfortunately, I don't remember her name. She was from New York. I was interviewed by Gordon

Peterson. He interviewed us about the drought in the Sahel. It lasted for about 10 or 15 minutes.

So, Luke was in Diffa and I got a call. We had this little office, and I don't remember the fellow's name, but he was our secretary. I got this call, and he said, "Joe, this fellow from the Lilly Endowment is going to be in Washington, coming from New York and he wants to meet with us, with *Africare*."

What had happened was that this lady who had been on television with me - and here's where connections and support comes about - Charles Williams who was the Senior Vice President of the Lilly Endowment asked her if there were any organizations that were doing anything in Africa at that time. She said yes. She told him she had been on this program "with this fellow named Joe Kennedy from *Africare* and I think you should contact them." So he was coming from New York, and he did come.

He had already met with a group in New York. They were trying to start something, but somehow it didn't vibrate. Fortunately, Oumarou was out of town, so we were able to use his nice office and then we met with Charles Williams.

Canaan: Oumarou at this time, his position was what?

Dr. Kennedy: He was the Charge d'Affairs. He was not the Ambassador. He was the number two person in the embassy. But Oumarou was out of town. Rather than using our tiny office, we used his nice office. We met with Charles Williams. Charles Williams, as I said, was the Vice President of the Lilly Endowment, and the Lilly Endowment had never really done anything internationally. However, Charles Williams had this interest in Africa. So we met and he said, "Well, if you had some money, what would you do with it? If you had $50,000 or $100,000, how would you use it to help the refugees?" I told him that we would deepen and dig water wells rather than distributing food. We would dig these water wells, because, even though we can't prevent the drought, there is water there in the ground. If we draw it up and put in wells, when another drought comes, they'll have water. He really liked that idea. He asked us to give him a proposal for about $250,000. I said, "Okay, great." He asked how soon he could have it. I think this was like on a Monday. I said, "Well you can have it by Wednesday [chuckling]." And he said, "Give it to me by the end of the week." The next day, I took off from the Department of Education and sat there with, I think his name was John, the secretary, and we drew up this proposal for putting in water wells. And we were going to do it in three countries, Mali, Niger, and Upper Volta.

Then Luke came back, and I said, "Hey man, guess what? We have $250,000." He couldn't believe it. This all happened when he was in Africa. This was in the latter part of 1973. It had been June or July when Sam Stokes and I had gone there with the $60,000. So we got this grant from the Lilly Endowment through Charles Williams in late 1973. That was our first big job. Things took off. We started getting money. We kept expanding until eventually we were in thirty-six countries. And since the formation of *Africare*, we've raised and spent nearly two billion dollars. In 1999 I retired from *Africare*. I remain on the board and *Africare* is still going.

—

My grandfather dedicated his life to helping others and he often tells me that if I can dramatically impact or change even just one person's life in positive way then I have made a difference. My grandfather never wanted to be in the spotlight, he didn't want everyone to know his name. He wanted to help those less fortunate than himself. He didn't do it for the money, he was selfless and to this day he doesn't glorify what he has done. My grandfather is a humble and honorable man and I have always been proud to call him my grandfather and I wanted people to know of his contributions to this world.

Family Influences

My grandfather's family played a powerful role in his dreams and achievements. I wanted to briefly mention members of his family because they too influenced me to write this book.

JAMES ATKINS
May 7, 1890 -August 8, 1968

James Atkins was born in Knoxville, Tennessee. He was the brother of my great-grandmother Cara Atkins Kennedy. His father died when he was ten making him responsible for helping his mother sustain their lives. He worked on many jobs and finally got a job doing errands for a printing press, which led to his lifelong love of writing. His book, *Age of Jim Crow*, chronicles his life of humanitarian work, including his time as a member of President Franklin D. Roosevelt's "Black Cabinet," advising on committees formed to understand the plight of black people in America and how they could best be educated and given economic power. He was a pioneer in the Colorado school system, writing *Human Relations in Colorado 1858-1959*. He devoted his life to exploring and trying to solve racial disparity and discord in America. Every morning he had breakfast in his Colorado dining room on a white linen cloth with the china silverware perfectly laid. At breakfast he was dressed in a suit and tie as he read the Denver Post.

MARY KENNEDY CARTER
January 13, 1934 – December 14, 2010

Mary Kennedy Carter was born in Franklin, Ohio. My great aunt Mary Kennedy Carter's biggest accomplishment was her work on a committee to reveal the truth behind slavery in New York. She grew up in Ohio youngest of six children. She became valedictorian of her class and went on to graduate from Ohio State just as all of her siblings had done. In 1970, Mary Kennedy published *On to Freedom* about a slave family's planned escape from the south. She soon moved to New York and got a job for Mcgraw-Hill for a short time, then became an adjunct professor at Hofstra. There she became apart of a small group of professors who created the New York and Slavery: Complicity and Resistance curriculum. This curr-iculum won the Program of Excellence Award in 2005.

JAMES SCOTT KENNEDY
December 8, 1921- July 28, 2005

My great uncle James was born in Knoxville, Tennessee but grew up in Franklin, Ohio. Their family grew up in a small house during the depression; food was scarce and many nights he would go to bed hungry. The schools in Franklin were almost all white and dealing with discrimination and racism was an everyday affair. James Kennedy reflects on racism in his book *In Search of African Theatre*, "I have been called many things, including Colored, Afro-American, Black, Negro, Boy, Nigger and on a rare occasion, American."

After graduating from high school, James Kennedy went to work in a CCC [Civilian Conservation Corps] camp which provided men with jobs restoring nature sites. There he learned how to box, gaining the skills which he used later to pay for his college tuition. He fought as a welterweight, fighting in over 40 professional fights.

He enrolled at New York University in the 1940's. While in New York he struggled to make it, with very little financial support from his family. He had to work long and vigorous hours while being an exceptional student. He lived at the Harlem YMCA while he earned extra money as a manager at the famed nightclub, Smalls Paradise. He went on to receive his PhD from NYU in Theater. He became a senior tenured professor at Brooklyn College while pursuing his interest in African theatre. "My home was filled with both spiritual and religious vibrations and the richness of music, poetry and dramatic experiences", he stated. "My search for theatre started during my childhood."

LEON KENNEDY II
1920, ? -June 4, 1948

Leon Kennedy was the oldest child of Leon and Cara Kennedy, my great grandparents. They had six children, Leon, James, Joseph, Irene, Lillian and Mary. Leon was their lead -er. Leon worked during high school trying to put food on the table for his brothers and sisters. He was an amateur boxer, training at the local gym whenever he got the chance. His brother James and himself were called the "Battling Brothers". Leon would enter the ring and knock out his opponent and his brother would come out after him and knockout his opponent. They were unbeatable.

When World War II broke out Leon and James volunteered for service. They went to an examination office where they would be weighed and measured to see if they were fit for duty. They were the only black men there. All of the officers were white. They were asked to take an I.Q test. Leon got a perfect score; the white officer assumed he cheated and forced him to take it again. Again, Leon got a perfect score. The officer was in a daze, he couldn't believe a black could ace the test. They both ended up being sent home because of some "irregularity" the military did not disclose to Leon or James. After high school Leon attended Howard University. He was the forerunner for the family, the first of the kids to go to college. Leon trained as a boxer and his dream was to be the first professional boxer with a degree in medicine. After two years at Howard he transferred to New York University. At age twenty eight Leon was going to be a father, to have a child with a woman whom he fell in love with while in New York. Three days after the birth of his son Leon Kennedy III, Leon was going for a run in the park when his heart gave out. He had a heart attack. Leon was doing boxing road work before joining Heavyweight Champion Joe Louis' training camp to be a sparring partner. He died in that park, never to fulfill his dream of becoming a doctor. He was the leader of the family, the first one of the kids to go to college, they looked up to him. Leon's death was a tragedy but instead of dwelling on his death the Kennedy children persevered and the remaining five children all graduated from college, three earning their PhDs.

Dr. Joseph Kennedy speaks about his brother Leon Kennedy.

Canaan: One last thing I want to ask you about is your brother Leon, if you could tell me what you remember about him?

Dr. Kennedy: Well, now we were just in this little town in Franklin, 25,000 people. About maybe 60 black people, and there's nothing to do in Franklin. So when Leon graduated from high school, they say he was only ninety seven pounds because we didn't have any food. This was a time with Joe Louis, who was "The Man".

All the black people, the young men are going to be boxers emulating Joe Louis, "The Brown Bomber", so Leon and James would get out with their friends, put on the boxing gloves and box. So Leon was going to escape Franklin through boxing, but in the meantime there was one of these Roosevelt [President Franklin D. Roosevelt] programs called the Civilian Conservation Corps, CCC's. It created jobs for young people, men out of work. They would conserve the trees and build the roads and so on. So Leon joined the CCC camp and then that got him out of Franklin.

James followed in the CCC camp. Leon was going to make his breakout through boxing and they were called the "BBs, the Battling Brothers," and Leon would come out and box and win and James would come out and box and win. Leon decided to go to Washington, but he was still boxing. Our Uncle James lived in Washington. James boxed for a little while and gave it up but Leon was going to make his money and his fortune through boxing. And so he boxed I think he boxed in Griffith stadium. I think they changed the name. But he boxed there and I saw him and I'd go and watch him train and carry his little bag. I think I was still in high school when I would go there for the summer.

Canaan: Was he going to school?

Joseph Kennedy: Howard.

Canaan: Okay. Tell me about Leon's death.

Joseph Kennedy: I was at Ohio State when I got the word that Leon had died of a heart attack in Prospect Park in Brooklyn. He was out running. One of the park attendants saw him and thought he was resting. But he was dead.

In Conclusion

I have learned from these interviews how race influences our lives not just in America but around the world. Even though the circumstances of my father's childhood were very different, he like my grandfather still had to deal with racial problems. In New York, where he lived most of the time he was often confronted with negative racial attitudes.

Almost every day since I can remember my father would tell me stories of the great struggle that our ancestors had to go through. After years and years of listening to his lectures I finally decided to do something with all that knowledge I had gained. I decided I wanted to write a book about all the stories I had heard sitting at the dinner table every night. I wanted the world to know who I was, who my family was and the struggles they went through in life.

As I have said, I have struggled with being an interracial child. I would question my family and often wonder if I were adopted because I was so light skinned. After accepting who I was, I wanted to show everyone who my family was.

Understanding how my family dealt with difficult situations and how they persevered through tough times has always interested me because I too want to be able to make it through life and be able to overcome any and all hardships.

I had an epiphany one day to sit down and actually start writing the book. I can't tell you what compelled me to do so, but this drive inside of me pushed me everyday to work on it.

I hope my families' stories can help you navigate through life like they have helped me.

BIOGRAPHY

Canaan Kennedy is a freshman at VCU, Virginia Commonwealth University. In the past year he has produced interviews and conducted a survey on racial relationships at his school. He also has conducted several interviews with his family about their work and views on the world. He is pursuing a double major in English and African American Studies. One of his role models is Fareed Zakaria. He was a member of the Model UN and Forensics Club at his high school. He enjoys lectures on literature and is an avid football fan.

Canaan Kennedy High School Graduation 2015.

58799460R00063

Made in the USA
Charleston, SC
19 July 2016